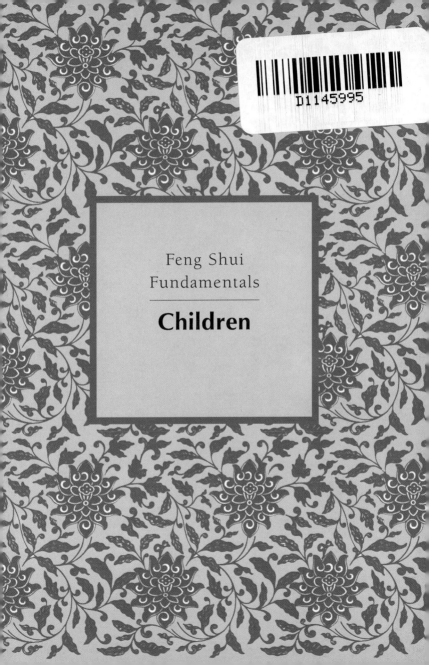

Feng Shui
Fundamentals

Children

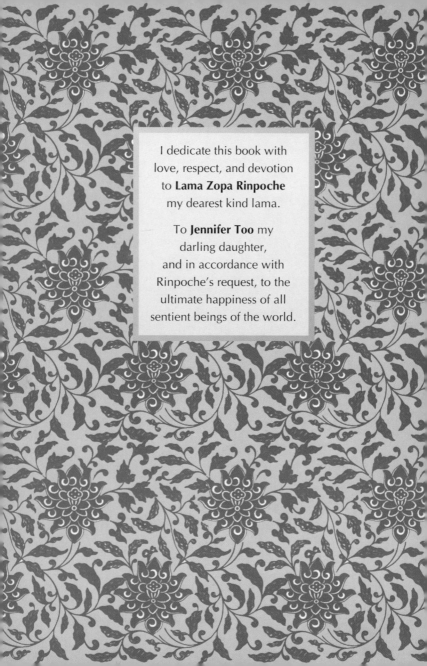

I dedicate this book with
love, respect, and devotion
to **Lama Zopa Rinpoche**
my dearest kind lama.

To **Jennifer Too** my
darling daughter,
and in accordance with
Rinpoche's request, to the
ultimate happiness of all
sentient beings of the world.

Feng Shui
Fundamentals

Children

Lillian Too

ELEMENT

Shaftesbury, Dorset • Rockport, Massachusetts • Melbourne, Victoria

© Element Books Limited 1997
Text © Lillian Too 1997

First published in Great Britain by
ELEMENT BOOKS LIMITED
Shaftesbury, Dorset SP7 8BP

Published in the USA in 1997 by
ELEMENT BOOKS INC.
PO Box 830, Rockport, MA 01966

Published in Australia in 1997 by
ELEMENT BOOKS LIMITED
and distributed by Penguin Australia Ltd
487 Maroondah Highway, Ringwood, Victoria 3134

Designed and created with
THE BRIDGEWATER BOOK COMPANY LIMITED

ELEMENT BOOKS LIMITED
Editorial Director Julia McCutchen
Managing Editor Caro Ness
Production Director Roger Lane
Production Sarah Golden

THE BRIDGEWATER BOOK COMPANY LIMITED
Art Director Terry Jeavons
Designer James Lawrence
Managing Editor Anne Townley
Project Editor Andrew Kirk
Editor Linda Doeser
Picture Research Julia Hanson
Studio Photography Guy Ryecart
Illustrations Isabel Rayner, Andrew Kulman, Mark Jamieson,
Michaela Blunden, Paul Collicutt, Olivia Rayner, Jackie Harland

Printed and bound in Hong Kong

British Library Cataloguing in Publication Data available

Library of Congress Cataloging in Publication data available

ISBN 1 86204 123 7

The publishers wish to thank the following for the use of pictures:
Bridgeman Art Library, p 34: Elizabeth Whiting Associates, pp 47, 50; e.t. archive, p 11;
Julia Hanson, p 43; Image Bank, pp 8, 16; and Zefa, pp 15, 18, 19, 32, 46.

Special thanks go to:
Bright Ideas, Lewes, East Sussex
for help with properties

Lillian Too's website addresses are
http://www.asiaconnect.com.my/lillian-too
http://www.dragonmagic.com

Lillian Too's email addresses are
ltoo@dragonmagic.com
ltoo@popmail.asiaconnect.com.my

CONTENTS

INTRODUCTION TO FENG SHUI

WHAT IS FENG SHUI ?

風水

For centuries, the Chinese have attributed the well-being of families to the intangible forces that surround their homes. They refer to this as feng shui, literally translated as "wind and water". The success and happiness of families were believed to result from living in homes that had good feng shui or a balanced environment, while a lack of descendants and other misfortunes were ascribed to harmful feng shui. Auspicious feng shui requires the family home to be built and arranged according to favorable orientations, so that the home and its residents benefit from the positive energies of the environment. These energies are invisible and intangible, but they exert powerful influences.

THE COSMIC BREATH

Feng shui describes these energies as a kind of life force, termed chi, or the cosmic breath. Chi can be beneficial and auspicious, bringing material benefits and great good fortune, in which case it is called sheng chi. It can also be harmful and injurious. This killing breath, termed shar chi, brings huge misfortune, sickness, loss, and immense bad luck. Sometimes it even brings death. Feng shui teaches us how to attract the good sheng chi and avoid the bad shar chi.

Harnessing sheng chi involves placing objects, arranging furniture, and orienting homes and offices according to feng shui guidelines. Protecting the home from shar chi entails diagnosing furniture arrangements and orientations that are harmful. It requires rearrangment of doors and furniture to deflect this killing breath or

FUTURE GENERATIONS

This book explains how feng shui can be used to enhance your descendants-luck. The emphasis is on the next generation – how to use feng shui to improve your children's luck in study, work, and love. Childless couples can also improve their chances of starting a family with feng shui.

the use of special feng shui cures that cause the killing breath to be dissolved.

Feng shui is neither magical nor spiritual. There are diverse components of superstition and symbolism in the practice, but this is because feng shui is a very old science whose origins go back at least 3,000 years. The theoretical foundation of feng shui is based on the Chinese view of the universe. Much of this was documented in ancient texts, but a great deal more has come down the centuries by word of mouth, passed from father to son. This has given the practice heavy superstitious overtones that have sometimes become confused with traditional and spiritual practices. This was mainly due to feng shui's observed potency in improving the material well-being of those who followed its guidelines.

Feng shui addresses almost the entire spectrum of human aspiration. The practice operates at various levels. It can be highly personalized when practiced according to specific compass school formulas, or it can be broad based and

Applying feng shui guidelines to your living space can improve your children's prospects in life.

generalized. There are different schools of practice resulting from variations in the interpretation of ancient texts and by the differences in dialect in feng shui source books or materials.

The methods used in this book are based on both the form and the compass school. The former method involves interpretation of the terrain, contours, shapes, topography, elevation, rivers, and waterways, while compass feng shui offers recommendations in terms of compass directions. Neither method is more or less important than the others and usually a combination of methods is used to create the best results. It is never possible to get everything right with feng shui and it is impossible to follow every recommendation that might be suggested. As long as you can implement about 60 percent of recommendations, your feng shui can be said to be good.

THE CHINESE VIEW
OF DESCENDANTS-LUCK

In the avenue of stone figures leading to the tombs of the Ming emperors just outside Beijing, there are gigantic stone monoliths of standing and kneeling elephants, which are believed to bring immeasurable descendants-luck to childless women. Placing a stone on the back of one of these elephants, it was believed, would ensure the birth of a male child.

The new brides of prominent families were often given lavish servings of pomegranates to symbolize the family's hope for numerous male offspring who would rise to glory and fame. The pomegranate was said to be an emblem of great fertility because it has so many seeds.

One of the stone elephants along the Spirit Road leading to the Ming Tombs near Beijing, China. They are associated with good descendants-luck.

Luck with descendants has always been of such prime importance to the Chinese that feng shui has merged strongly with superstition in the myriad beliefs and practices that address this universal aspiration of Chinese families. Indeed, if there were no sons to take the family into the next generation, it was interpreted as the worst kind of bad luck. The marriage bed was often decorated with all the symbols of fertility,and young virgin boys born in

the dragon year were asked to roll across the bed in the belief that this would imbue it with the auspicious spirit of sturdy offspring for the newlyweds. Embroidered curtains and sheets, vases, and paintings of children would be strategically placed in the bedroom with the same purpose in view.

References to offspring in the Chinese culture referred almost exclusively to sons. Daughters were not counted and even in modern China, sons are far more welcome than daughters. This is mainly because sons carry on the family name. Daughters were said to leave the family upon marriage, while sons brought home daughters-in-law.

In the old textbooks on feng shui, luck was often described in terms of the number of sons a certain orientation would bring and ill luck was described in terms of the loss of sons. Descendants-luck thus features prominently in the practice of feng shui. It is even stated in some of these texts that where the astrological birth chart predicts a lack of descendants, this could be overcome with good feng shui. The luck could be sufficiently manipulated to produce one son or, perhaps, present the couple with a consolation prize – the birth of female children instead!

At one time in China, the birth of a son was so important a part of the marriage purpose that wives who could not fulfill this aspect of their role were often discarded. Husbands could cite the non-production of male offspring as sufficient excuse to install a secondary wife.

Auspicious descendants-luck, however, also means that children will be filial, virtuous, and obedient – and Chinese folk tales are peppered with stories of filial devotion, duty, and obedience. Good feng shui can help ensure that families enjoy exactly this kind of good fortune and there is specific advice offered in the feng shui texts that addresses this dimension of family luck.

Fertility symbolism was an important feature of the Chinese marriage bed.

FENG SHUI FOR THE NEXT GENERATION

THE MAIN TOOLS OF FENG SHUI

The Luo Pan is the main reference tool of feng shui practitioners. This circular geomantic compass, usually made of wood, is painted red and gold and contains multiple rings of Chinese characters that represent the meanings and symbols associated with the directions of the compass. It is still used by many modern feng shui consultants in Asia, although for accuracy of readings, many also supplement this traditional tool with modern, Western-style compasses.

The Luo Pan has a compass in the center where the needle points south. This is in keeping with the Chinese tradition of placing south at the top. However, in practice, this south is exactly the same south as that indicated by any Western compass. The north of feng shui is also the same magnetic north referred to in Western compass terminology. The first of the concentric rings on the Luo Pan compass divides space into eight directions, made up of the four cardinal directions – north, south, east, and west – and four secondary directions – southwest, southeast, northwest, and northeast.

Immediately adjacent to the compass are the relevant matching trigrams. There are a total of eight basic trigrams and these are arranged round the Luo Pan according to the way they are placed around the Pa Kua (see pages 12–18). These trigrams offer powerful meanings to the directions and form much of the fundamental basis of feng shui practice.

The Luo Pan also divides space into 24 sub-categories of directions. There are three sub-directions for every main direction, therefore making a total of 24. To expose their true potency, many of the advanced formulas of feng shui require extreme accuracy when taking directions. There then follows element notations and

TIP

For the amateur practitioner, a Western boy scout compass is usually good enough. In fact, it is preferable for convenience as well as accuracy.

further concentric rings of other codes and symbols. The more advanced the feng shui practice, the larger the number of rings on the Luo Pan compass!

In practical feng shui, the Luo Pan compass can be applied to a room, home, an entire building, a complex of buildings, a city, and even a country. The exact codes often differ according to which Master's feng shui method is being applied and old feng shui Masters often have their own codes and notes written on their personal Luo Pans, which are then carefully guarded and kept secret from others.

For amateur practitioners, the Luo Pan is not necessary. It is sufficient to use a conventional compass to identify directions and to understand the relationship between trigrams, elements, and directions. This simplifies the practice tremendously, but this simplicity of approach is nevertheless just as potent.

The Luo Pan has the compass in the center. It is surrounded by concentric rings of Chinese characters and symbols that represent the codes and reference tools of the feng shui Master. Advanced Masters of the science often have their own Luo Pans that contain their personal trade secrets.

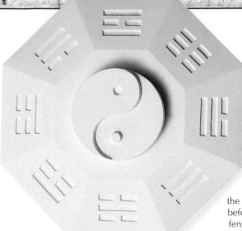

The eight-sided Pa Kua should always be placed with the south at the top before it is used for feng shui diagnosis

THE PA KUA AND THE LO SHU SQUARE

The feng shui compass derives much of its meanings from the eight-sided Pa Kua symbol. Each side represents one of the eight directions of the compass and, in accordance with Chinese tradition, the direction south is placed at the top. This placement is significant since the meanings and attributes of all the directions are determined from the eight trigrams placed round the Pa Kua. It is thus important in feng shui to make the correct association between directions and trigrams. Once this first important connection has been made, we can start to activate the five elements (see pages 17–19).

Practical feng shui thus involves studying directions, trigrams, and elements and then implementing the interpretations of the relationships between these three important reference tools. It is very easy to study and understand how to apply them in a practical manner. This is the basic approach and, once these fundamental principles have been mastered, it then becomes increasingly easy to probe more deeply, finding further layers of meaning in the Pa Kua.

There are two arrangements of the trigrams around the Pa Kua: the Early Heaven Arrangement and the Later Heaven Arrangement. The Pa Kua of the Later Heaven Arrangement is shown here. This is always the arrangement used when diagnosing the feng shui of yang dwellings, in other words, the houses of the living. Under this arrangement, Tui, the trigram that represents children, joy, and the next generation is placed in the west, and so it is the west that must be energized to activate luck for your children which the Chinese call descendants-luck.

THE LO SHU SQUARE

A second important tool of feng shui is the Lo Shu square. This is a nine-sector grid, each sector of which contains a number from one to nine. The numbers are arranged in the grid so that the sum of any three numbers, horizontally, vertically, and diagonally, is 15, which is also the number of days it takes the moon to grow from new to full. The Chinese believe this is a magic square and that it provides the key to unlocking many of the secrets of the Pa Kua.

The amateur practitioner should be completely familiar with the Lo Shu and its arrangement of numbers in order to understand how to use it with the Pa Kua. Since we have identified the west as the most important direction to activate children's luck, we will discover that when we superimpose the Lo Shu square onto the Pa Kua, the number corresponding to the direction west is seven. This is also the number that represents the present period from 1984 to 2003. In this 20-year period, the number seven represents extreme good fortune. Therefore correctly activating this number in the west would be most auspicious, especially for the younger members of the family.

It is believed that the Lo Shu square appeared several thousand years ago on the back of a turtle that emerged from the River Lo. This square features prominently in feng shui technology, particularly in some of the more advanced feng shui formulas.

ENERGIZING THE PA KUA FOR CHILDREN'S LUCK

Activating your children's luck starts with understanding the Pa Kua. By itself, the Pa Kua of the Early Heaven Arrangement is believed to be a powerful protective tool. Merely hanging it outside the home above the main door is deemed very effective in countering any negative energies that may be threatening the home and its residents.

However, the Pa Kua, with its aggregated circles of meaning, is also a feng shui reference tool. There is meaning in each of the trigrams placed at every edge of it. Trigrams are three-lined symbols. The lines may be solid yang or broken yin lines and their relationship is what gives meaning to the trigrams, according to the I Ching, the Book of Changes.

The trigram that represents the next generation is Tui and, according to the Later Heaven Arrangement, this is placed in the west. This is the corner of any home or room that represents the luck of the children. If this corner has good feng shui, the children will enjoy excellent fortune: they will do well in school, achieve good grades, win honors, and excel in all their pursuits. If they enjoy good birth charts, the good feng shui will also assist them in attaining great heights in any endeavor.

However, if this corner has bad feng shui, bad luck will prevail and parents will find it difficult to help their children. The

Using feng shui to activate your children's luck will result in a happy and creative atmosphere.

children themselves will suffer from every kind of misfortune, from not doing well at school to constantly falling sick, They will find it difficult and sometimes impossible to achieve their potential despite their best efforts. Bad feng shui in this corner creates tension between parents and their children and, at its worst, leads to parents

TUI

This trigram, made up of one broken yin line above two unbroken yang lines, signifies joyousness, laughter, and a time for rejoicing. The Tui trigram implies success and continuity of the family name. Seasonally, it represents fall and its symbol is the lake.

More than anything, Tui means gold, but not ordinary gold. The reference is metaphorical, for gold here means virtuous offspring who bring fame, honor, and happiness to the family. Good children are regarded as being as precious as gold. When the trigram Tui is activated, there is harmony in the family. Siblings enjoy good relationships and children respect the elders of the family. Husbands and wives get along and the atmosphere in the home is one of serenity.

The positive side of this trigram also suggests that families will be enlarged through marriage or having children.

who are completely unable to communicate with their children, and young people who are unsettled and who get into one scrape after another.

In order to maximize children's luck, feng shui requires careful examination of this sector of the room or home and in particular the meaning of the trigram Tui.

The Summer Palace of the Forbidden City in Beijing.
Feng shui guidelines were strictly applied to the design of the palaces
to activate the most auspicious energies for the heir to the throne.

THE DIRECTION EAST

Children's luck is also represented by the direction east, since this is the direction that symbolizes the unity of the family. The trigram of the east is Chen. To some schools of feng shui, Chen is far more indicative of sons, since this trigram symbolizes the eldest son. Activating the east corner of the home or of the living room is thus believed to be of great benefit to the eldest son of the family.

CHEN

The Chen trigram has two yin lines above one unbroken yang line: the yang symbolically pushes upward from below. Its intrinsic symbol is thunder and its characteristics encompass feelings that are associated with things that are arousing: movement, excitement, and strength. The season indicated is spring and the animal of this direction is, of course, the celestial dragon.

These are powerful symbols in feng shui since spring is the season of growth and the dragon is the main celestial creature associated with feng shui. In the Forbidden City, the palaces located in the east were those set aside for the young princes. All the symbols needed to activate this sector for great good fortune for the heir to the throne were carefully worked into roof and room designs. For example, the roof tiles of these palaces were green. This was because the east is of the wood element whose auspicious color is green. Adherence to these feng shui guidelines was most seriously applied during the reign of Ch'ien-lung.

THE FIVE ELEMENTS

The recommended method of energizing the directions that benefit children is to apply the theory and significance of the five elements. According to almost every one of the classical texts on feng shui, the theory of the five elements transcends almost every branch of feng shui practice. All things in the universe, tangible or intangible, are said to belong to one of five elements: fire, wood, water, metal, and earth. Each of the eight compass directions is said to represent one of these elements.

▨ The west is symbolized by the element small metal.
▨ The east is symbolized by the element big wood.
▨ The element of the south is fire.
▨ The element of the north is water.
▨ The element of the southwest is big earth.
▨ The element of the southeast is small wood.
▨ The element of the northwest is big metal.
▨ The element of the northwest is small earth.

Each element has its intrinsic characteristics, and the Chinese use element interpretation in all their divinatory sciences. In feng shui, understanding the significance of the elements in the various corners of the home is a vital component of effective and correct practice.

The element assigned to each of the directions is based on the corresponding trigram of the directions, which, in turn, is based on the arrangement of the trigrams according to the Later Heaven Arrangement.

PRINCIPLES OF FENG SHUI

THE CYCLES OF THE FIVE ELEMENTS

Applying element analysis to feng shui practice requires an understanding of the nature of their interactions with each other. According to the theory, there are two cycles that form the basis of element interpretation. These are the productive and the destructive cycles. The five elements interact with each other and move in never-ending positive and negative cycles.

The universal corner identified with children's luck is the west for which the element is metal. The northern Chinese schools of feng shui, however, also consider the east beneficial for children, since this is the family luck corner. The element of the east is wood.

LUCK

One method of activating luck for the children of the family requires the following three steps

▨ Identify the corner of the home and its rooms that represent children.

▨ Check the corresponding element of the corner(s) identified.

▨ Activate the corner using elements as a guide.

PRODUCTIVE CYCLE

This illustration shows the productive cycle of the five elements – earth, metal, water, wood, and fire. Earth, the element that produces metal, is in a positive position in relation to metal and is therefore helping to energize metal, which is associated with children's luck.

DESTRUCTIVE CYCLE

This illustration shows the destructive cycle of the five elements. Metal is being overwhelmed by fire, the element that destroys metal. This means that metal, which is associated with children's luck, is not being strengthened.

THE METAL ELEMENT OF THE WEST

The ruling element of the west is metal, symbolized by all things made of metal, particularly gold. This includes metal windchimes, home appliances, televisions, and clocks. Identifying the relevant element to activate is a vital part of feng shui application. For instance, a windchime in the west part of the living room will activate excellent opportunities for the children of the family.

From these attributes, we know that to strengthen the element of the west, we

---

METAL

Examination of five element cycles reveals various characteristics of the metal element.

- Metal is produced by earth, so earth is said to be good for it.
- Metal itself produces water, so water is said to exhaust it.
- Metal is destroyed by fire, so fire is said to be harmful to it.
- Metal destroys wood, so it is said to overcome wood.

---

can use any objects that symbolize either earth or metal elements, but that we should avoid anything belonging to the fire element. This means that the west may be activated by any object, color, or painting that suggests either earth or metal. Electrical appliances that are made of metal and are placed in the west corner of a room would be harmonious. The display of windchimes and bells is also excellent, as are television sets and music systems. It is also auspicious to display objects that belong to the earth element, such as crystals, clay pots, and rocks.

USING OBJECTS OF THE METAL ELEMENT

Energizing the west is said to enhance the life force that brings auspicious benefits to children. Placing metal objects in the west of any room, or in the room which represents the west corner of the home, attracts the beneficial sheng chi that ensures children do well in their studies and careers. In practical feng shui this means placing household objects and appliances according to feng shui principles and incorporating the attributes and symbols of the metal element into the decoration of the room.

Display the family silver in a glass-fronted cabinet placed against the west wall of the living room, set up the television or stereo system there, or hang a clock on that wall. You can set up the computer terminal in the west corner of the study. Make sure the wall that represents this direction is painted white, since this is the color that symbolizes metal.

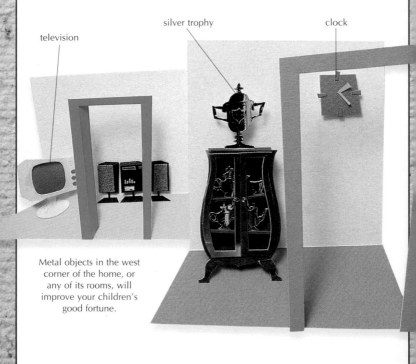

television

silver trophy

clock

Metal objects in the west corner of the home, or any of its rooms, will improve your children's good fortune.

USING OBJECTS WITH ADDITIONAL FENG SHUI SIGNIFICANCE

The sound of bells attract good sheng chi and activate your children's luck.

There are other objects that have greater feng shui significance. Perhaps one of the most effective feng shui energizers is a windchime that is made of metal. A bell is another favorite object of good fortune, deemed most suitable for activating auspicious children's luck. The Chinese place dragon bells on the west side of their rooms to summon the family to dinner. Bells are also considered good feng shui because their sound attracts the good sheng chi. Any kind of bell is acceptable, but it is a good idea to look for decorative ones made of brass, which emit attractive sounds that bring good feng shui. Bells are also excellent energizers when hung on the door handles of main doors. This is also believed to enhance business luck.

THE WINDCHIME

Made of several hollow rods tied together, the windchime is said to be very effective in channeling sheng chi upwards. The tinkling sounds of the rods as they move in the wind are said to encourage the auspicious life force to accumulate and settle, bringing good fortune to the household. Windchimes with solid rods are ineffective as feng shui energizers. In Chinese homes, windchimes made of copper and fashioned into pagodas and stars are very popular because the Chinese also believe that the windchime by itself is an auspicious object to have in the home. Place the chime in the west to create good luck for the children, but do not overdo it. One windchime is sufficient.

THE WOOD ELEMENT OF THE EAST

The symbolic element of the east is wood and the best representation of it is living plants and flowers. Since east is regarded as the corner that affects family luck, activating east walls, corners, and even the roof will attract precious sheng chi to the home – the sort that brings happiness and luck to the children of the family. Their success and well-being will be improved vastly and there will be more respect from the children for their parents, and better communication from everyone.

When energizing wood, you should consider the attributes of this element in relation to the others.

- ▓ Wood is produced by water, so water is said to be good for it.
- ▓ Wood itself produces fire, so fire is said to exhaust it.
- ▓ Wood is destroyed by metal, so metal is said to be harmful to it.
- ▓ Wood destroys earth, so it is said to overcome earth.

These relationships indicate that the east can, in effect, be energized by objects that belong to both the wood and water elements. It also suggests that placing objects of the metal element in the east, such as televisions or computers, or even windchimes, will destroy the intrinsic forces of the corner with disastrous results.

CACTUS AND BONSAI

Cactus and bonsai plants should be avoided. No matter how stunning they may look, resist the temptation to have them in your home, let alone in the east corner.

It is an excellent idea to combine the wood and water elements. Display a bowl of water lilies or place freshly cut flowers in a vase. Fresh flowers are always excellent feng shui, as they represent life and wonderful yang energy (but throw them away as soon as they wilt or the energy will stagnate).

Cactus has thorns that emit harmful shar chi and bonsai represents stunted growth, an unwanted symbolism, especially for children.

ACTIVATING WOOD INSIDE THE HOME

This can be done by displaying indoor plants. Place them on window sills to catch the morning sun and make sure they look healthy and luscious. Dying and sickly plants are bad feng shui and they should be thrown out and immediately replaced with healthy ones. Artificial plants are acceptable although live plants are better. However, dried flowers emit too much yin energy and so they do not represent good feng shui.

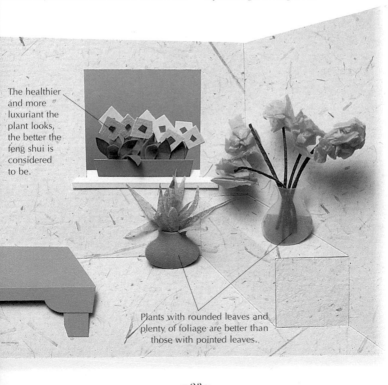

The healthier and more luxuriant the plant looks, the better the feng shui is considered to be.

Plants with rounded leaves and plenty of foliage are better than those with pointed leaves..

COLORS AND INTERIOR DECORATION

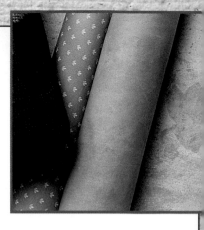

White and metallic colors are the ones to use for the west corners of rooms. Correct colors strengthen the element and create a good feng shui balance for the corner, benefiting the type of luck it signifies. This guideline is best followed in the family or living room, as these are the ones that are most in use.

Soft furnishings, such as drapes, rugs, and cushion covers, can be any color except red, since red is of the fire element and that destroys metal.

BLUES AND GREENS FOR THE EAST

The combination of the water and wood elements suggest blues and greens in all shades. Use light tones for the walls and let your creativity run riot for all the soft furnishings. Flowered designs on sofa covers and rugs are excellent. Avoid metallic colors, including silver and gold, since metal destroys wood. Also avoid geometric designs with sharp edges. Checks and stripes do not represent auspicious feng shui. Designs with pointed edges do the most harm.

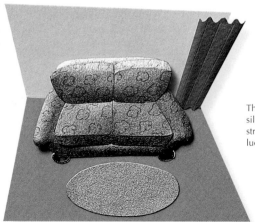

The metallic colors of silver and gold will strengthen the feng shui luck of west corners

MOTIFS AND DESIGNS

Wallpaper, drapes, rugs, and sofa covers can carry auspicious patterns that enhance the corners where they are placed. For the east, water, trees, flowers, or even the green dragon can be worked into designs. In the metal corners, motifs can incorporate gold or silver.

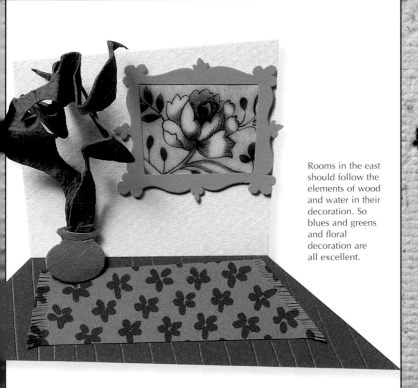

Rooms in the east should follow the elements of wood and water in their decoration. So blues and greens and floral decoration are all excellent.

ALLOCATING ROOMS ACCORDING TO THE TRIGRAMS

To get the best out of feng shui, allocate rooms to family members taking your cue from the trigrams around the Pa Kua of the Later Heaven Arrangement. This is appropriate for yang dwellings – the homes of the living as opposed to yin dwellings – homes for the dead.

The method of superimposing the nine-sector Lo Shu grid which divides the home into nine sectors, is described on pages 32–33, after which the directions should be taken with a compass.

ROOMS FOR THE FAMILY

According to the Pa Kua of the Later Heaven Arrangement, the eight directions of any living space that correspond to the eight directions of the compass are as follows:

- ▧ The northwest for the father.
- ▧ The southwest for the mother.
- ▧ The east for the eldest or only son.
- ▧ The southeast for the eldest or only daughter.
- ▧ The north for the middle son.
- ▧ The south for the middle daughter.
- ▧ The northeast for the youngest son.
- ▧ The west for the youngest daughter.

ROOMS FOR PARENTS

The parents, especially the father, can be located in the northwest because the trigram for this direction is Chien, which represents the father. Practitioners of feng shui can choose to locate the master bedroom according to this method or they can follow the compass formula, which offers personal best directions based on the date of birth (see page 28–29). The method used is often dependent on the home itself, as there is not always complete freedom of choice due to constraints of shape and space.

The southwest is represented by the trigram Kun, which signifies the matriarch. This direction would be well suited to house the family room, since the female maternal spirit cares for the welfare of the entire family.

ROOMS FOR CHILDREN

Ideally, the sons of the family should sleep in the room that corresponds to the east of the home. If there is more than one son, other suitable rooms for them are the north and northeast. The east is, however, the best place for all the sons of the family since the trigram here is Chen, which means successful growth.

The daughters of the family can be located with equal advantage in the southeast, the south, or the west. The favorite daughter (usually the youngest) is usually the one who sleeps in the west, since the trigram here is Tui, which means joyous and it also symbolizes young women.

Allocating rooms according to the trigrams of the Later Heaven Arrangement will ensure beneficial feng shui for the family.

Father in the northwest

Sons in the northeast or east

Mother in the southwest

Daughter in the southeast

COMPASS FENG SHUI FOR FAMILY LUCK

THE COMPASS FORMULA

Every member of the family can use this very powerful compass school formula to calculate the directions that are the most personally auspicious. The formula was a closely guarded secret for many years. Known as Pa Kua Lo Shu feng shui (or Kua formula), this method was given to the author's feng shui Master by a venerable and wise Taiwan feng shui Grand Master who was a legend in his time.

The formula was derived from the two ancient symbols of feng shui – the eight-sided Pa Kua, with its many levels of meanings, and the Lo Shu magic square, a nine-sector grid that is believed to be the key to unlocking the secrets of the Pa Kua. According to the feng shui masters, each person has four auspicious and four inauspicious directions, depending on whether they are east or west group people. The group you belong to is determined by your year of birth and gender.

The auspicious family direction of every person is known as the nien yen direction. Once you know your personal nien yen direction, you can make use of it to enhance your family luck through feng shui. You can use it with equal success in the various rooms of your home. Essentially this means sleeping and sitting in a direction that allows you to capture your auspicious direction, which attracts excellent luck in your relations with all members of your family.

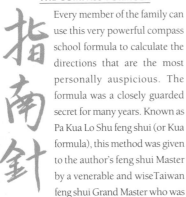

If your Kua number is:

1 east group

2 west group

3 east group

4 east group

5 west group

6 west group

7 west group

8 west group

9 east group

Activating the nien yen of your children helps them focus. The nien yen is a very powerful direction to activate if family luck is what you want. In addition to enhancing your descendants-luck, it will also prove beneficial to your marriage, and create greater family happiness.

THE KUA FORMULA

To determine your nien yen direction, first determine your Kua number as shown here. Obtain your Chinese year of birth based on the calendar on pages 30–31 and use this to calculate your Kua number.

Your Family orientation is:

SOUTH for both males and females

NORTHWEST for both males and females

SOUTHEAST for both males and females

EAST for both males and females

NORTHWEST for males and **WEST** for females

SOUTHWEST for both males and females

NORTHEAST for both males and females

WEST for both males and females

NORTH for both males and females

THE KUA FORMULA

Calculate your Kua number as follows.
Add the last two digits of your Chinese year of birth. e.g. **1957**, 5+7=**12**.
If the sum is higher than ten, reduce to a single digit, thus **1+2=3**.

Males	**Females**
Subtract from	Add
10	**5**
thus	thus
10-3	**5+3**
=7	**=8**
So, for men born in	So, for women born in
1957	**1957**
the Kua number is	the Kua number is
7	**8**

Now check against this table for your family direction and location.

Number 5 is not used in the Kua formula, although for clarity it is listed opposite. Females should use 8 instead of 5, and males 2.

THE CHINESE CALENDAR

Note that for the Chinese the New Year begins in either late January or early February. When calculating your Kua number do take note of this. Thus, if you are born in January 1946 before the New Year, your Chinese year of birth is 1945 and not 1946. This calendar also indicates the ruling element of your year of birth. This gives you further clues on which corner of the home will have the most effect on your well-being.

Year	From	To	Element	Year	From	To	Element
1900	31 Jan 1900	18 Feb 1901	Metal	1923	16 Feb 1923	4 Feb 1924	Water
1901	19 Feb 1901	17 Feb 1902	Metal	1924	5 Feb 1924	24 Jan 1925	Wood
1902	18 Feb 1902	28 Jan 1903	Water	1925	25 Jan 1925	12 Feb 1926	Wood
1903	29 Jan 1903	15 Jan 1904	Water	1926	13 Feb 1926	1 Feb 1927	Fire
1904	16 Feb 1904	3 Feb 1905	Wood	1927	2 Feb 1927	22 Jan 1928	Fire
1905	4 Feb 1905	24 Jan 1906	Wood	1928	23 Jan 1928	9 Feb 1929	Earth
1906	25 Jan 1906	12 Feb 1907	Fire	1929	10 Feb 1929	29 Jan 1930	Earth
1907	13 Feb 1907	1 Feb 1908	Fire	1930	30 Jan 1930	16 Feb 1931	Metal
1908	2 Feb 1908	21 Jan 1909	Earth	1931	17 Feb 1931	15 Feb 1932	Metal
1909	22 Jan 1909	9 Feb 1910	Earth	1932	16 Feb 1932	25 Jan 1933	Water
1910	10 Feb 1910	29 Jan 1911	Metal	1933	26 Jan 1933	13 Feb 1934	Water
1911	30 Jan 1911	17 Feb 1912	Metal	1934	14 Feb 1934	3 Feb 1935	Wood
1912	18 Feb 1912	25 Feb 1913	Water	1935	4 Feb 1935	23 Jan 1936	Wood
1913	26 Feb 1913	25 Jan 1914	Water	1936	24 Jan 1936	10 Feb 1937	Fire
1914	26 Jan 1914	13 Feb 1915	Wood	1937	11 Feb 1937	30 Jan 1938	Fire
1915	14 Feb 1915	2 Feb 1916	Wood	1938	31 Jan 1938	18 Feb 1939	Earth
1916	3 Feb 1916	22 Jan 1917	Fire	1939	19 Feb 1939	7 Feb 1940	Earth
1917	23 Jan 1917	10 Feb 1918	Fire	1940	8 Feb 1940	26 Jan 1941	Metal
1918	11 Feb 1918	31 Jan 1919	Earth	1941	27 Jan 1941	14 Feb 1942	Metal
1919	1 Feb 1919	19 Feb 1920	Earth	1942	15 Feb 1942	24 Feb 1943	Water
1920	20 Feb 1920	7 Feb 1921	Metal	1943	25 Feb 1943	24 Jan 1944	Water
1921	8 Feb 1921	27 Jan 1922	Metal	1944	25 Jan 1944	12 Feb 1945	Wood
1922	28 Jan 1922	15 Feb 1923	Water	1945	13 Feb 1945	1 Feb 1946	Wood

Year	From	To	Element	Year	From	To	Element
1946	2 Feb 1946	21 Jan 1947	Fire	1977	18 Feb 1977	6 Feb 1978	Fire
1947	22 Jan 1947	9 Feb 1948	Fire	1978	7 Feb 1978	27 Jan 1979	Earth
1948	10 Feb 1948	28 Jan 1949	Earth	1979	28 Jan 1979	15 Feb 1980	Earth
1949	29 Jan 1949	16 Feb 1950	Earth	1980	16 Feb 1980	4 Feb 1981	Metal
1950	17 Feb 1950	5 Feb 1951	Metal	1981	5 Feb 1981	24 Jan 1982	Metal
1951	6 Feb 1951	26 Jan 1952	Metal	1982	25 Jan 1982	12 Feb 1983	Water
1952	27 Jan 1952	13 Feb 1953	Water	1983	13 Feb 1983	1 Feb 1984	Water
1953	14 Feb 1953	2 Feb 1954	Water	1984	2 Feb 1984	19 Feb 1985	Wood
1954	3 Feb 1954	23 Jan 1955	Wood	1985	20 Feb 1985	8 Feb 1986	Wood
1955	24 Jan 1955	11 Feb 1956	Wood	1986	9 Feb 1986	28 Jan 1987	Fire
1956	12 Feb 1956	30 Jan 1957	Fire	1987	29 Jan 1987	16 Feb 1988	Fire
1957	31 Jan 1957	17 Feb 1958	Fire	1988	17 Feb 1988	5 Feb 1989	Earth
1958	18 Feb 1958	7 Feb 1959	Earth	1989	6 Feb 1989	26 Jan 1990	Earth
1959	8 Feb 1959	27 Jan 1960	Earth	1990	27 Jan 1990	14 Feb 1991	Metal
1960	28 Jan 1960	14 Feb 1961	Metal	1991	15 Feb 1991	3 Feb 1992	Metal
1961	15 Feb 1961	4 Feb 1962	Metal	1992	4 Feb 1992	22 Jan 1993	Water
1962	5 Feb 1962	24 Jan 1963	Water	1993	23 Jan 1993	9 Feb 1994	Water
1963	25 Jan 1963	12 Feb 1964	Water	1994	10 Feb 1994	30 Jan 1995	Wood
1964	13 Feb 1964	1 Feb 1965	Wood	1995	31 Jan 1995	18 Feb 1996	Wood
1965	2 Feb 1965	20 Jan 1966	Wood	1996	19 Feb 1996	7 Feb 1997	Fire
1966	21 Jan 1966	8 Feb 1967	Fire	1997	8 Feb 1997	27 Jan 1998	Fire
1967	9 Feb 1967	29 Jan 1968	Fire	1998	28 Jan 1998	15 Feb 1999	Earth
1968	30 Jan 1968	16 Feb 1969	Earth	1999	16 Feb 1999	4 Feb 2000	Earth
1969	17 Feb 1969	5 Feb 1970	Earth	2000	5 Feb 2000	23 Jan 2001	Metal
1970	6 Feb 1970	26 Jan 1971	Metal	2001	24 Jan 2001	11 Feb 2002	Metal
1971	27 Jan 1971	15 Feb 1972	Metal	2002	12 Feb 2002	31 Jan 2003	Water
1972	16 Feb 1972	22 Feb 1973	Water	2003	1 Feb 2003	21 Jan 2004	Water
1973	23 Feb 1973	22 Jan 1974	Water	2004	22 Jan 2004	8 Feb 2005	Wood
1974	23 Jan 1974	10 Feb 1975	Wood	2005	9 Feb 2005	28 Jan 2006	Wood
1975	11 Feb 1975	30 Jan 1976	Wood	2006	29 Jan 2006	17 Feb 2007	Fire
1976	31 Jan 1976	17 Feb 1977	Fire	2007	18 Feb 2007	6 Feb 2008	Fire

USING THE FORMULA

The layout of your home should be divided into the nine sectors according to the Lo Shu grid as shown. To do this accurately, use a good measuring tape and try to get the demarcations as accurate as possible. Next, get your bearings by identifying the eight corners according to the compass directions of each corner. Use a good compass (any western compass will do). Standing in the center of the home, identify the nine locations by dividing the total floor space into nine equal grids.

Draw out the floor plan of the home, as this will greatly assist you in arranging your rooms and furniture. This method of demarcating the home according to the Lo Shu square is an excellent way of identifying the corners of the home and can

BIG METAL

Northwest

SMALL METAL

West

BIG EARTH

Southwest

When using formula feng shui, it is essential to be very accurate in both your measurements and when taking compass directions. Note that rooms do not necessarily all fit neatly into the Lo Shu grid. Most rooms fall within two or even three sectors. This is when the exact placement of important pieces of furniture, such as desks and beds, becomes very important.

Descendants-luck means happy, healthy, and successful children and grandchildren.

WATER

North

EARTH

Northeast

BIG WOOD

East

FIRE

South

SMALL WOOD

Southeast

be used even when applying other feng shui methods.

To apply the formula, identify the corners that symbolize family luck – your nien yen corner. Remember that descendants-luck is most potent when based on the Kua number and directions of the head of the household, so you must identify their nien yen direction too.

Even as you identify the sectors of the home, always take note of their matching elements. This is because the application of the five elements theory transcends every school of feng shui and irrespective of the method or formula used, it is necessary to remember this. For ease of reference, the elements are indicated in each of the sectors. This is according to the Later Heaven Arrangement of the trigrams around the Pa Kua, the one that is always used in yang feng shui for the living. The element of the center is earth.

This gentle and beautiful sculpture which symbolizes parental love and mutual caring between parents and children would enhance the descendents luck of any home.

MATCHING HUMAN CHI TO ENVIRONMENTAL CHI

Once you know your personal family luck direction and you have demarcated the floor area of your house according to the Lo Shu square, there are several ways in which you can start to match your individual chi energies with that of your environment. You can activate your directions and attract auspicious sheng chi for the benefit of your whole family, especially if you are the main breadwinner.

Your Kua number, derived from the table on page 29, tells you your most auspicious direction for ensuring that you will not be lacking in children and descendants-luck. It also identifies the luckiest compass location for you to site your main door and your bedroom so as to make sure you capture smooth and harmonious sheng chi.

THE MASTER BEDROOM AND THE SLEEPING DIRECTION

Perhaps the best way of acquiring happy family luck is to try to match all the most important doors according to the nien yen directions of the people in your family who use the rooms, especially the bedrooms. If you are the breadwinner, you will need to sleep with your head pointed in your nien yen direction. This means locating the master bedroom in the nien yen sector.

EXAMPLE

If your nien yen direction is south, for instance, this is where your master bedroom should be located, and how your bed should be positioned, to tap your nien yen direction. This is the south corner of the home according to the compass. Since the nien yen direction is south, here is where the master bedroom should be located to tap auspicious luck for the whole family, and especially for conceiving a child. If you cannot get the location right, at least make certain you are sleeping with the top of your head pointed in your nien yen direction, in this case south.

FOR CHILDLESS COUPLES

If there is no known medical problem, when a man sleeps with the top of his head pointing to his personal nien yen direction, it will greatly enhance the couple's chances of conceiving a child. Indeed, this is one of the most wonderful benefits of practicing feng shui – the potential for bringing great joy and happiness to families.

The bedroom is located in the south of the house and the head of the bed is facing south

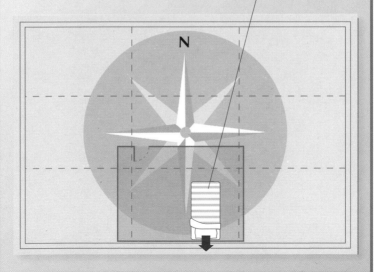

IRREGULAR-SHAPED HOMES

Homes rarely have regular, square, or rectangular shapes, making it difficult, in practice, to superimpose a nine-sector grid onto the floor layouts. However, a more serious problem is that of missing corners. If your nien yen corner is missing because of the shape of your home, then your family luck will be seriously undermined.

There are ways of getting round this problem and some are shown here, but correcting the problem merely improves the situation. It does not necessarily create the good family luck you seek.

You should first superimpose the nine-sector grid onto your house layout and, by taking directions from the center, it will be possible to see immediately which compass sector is missing.

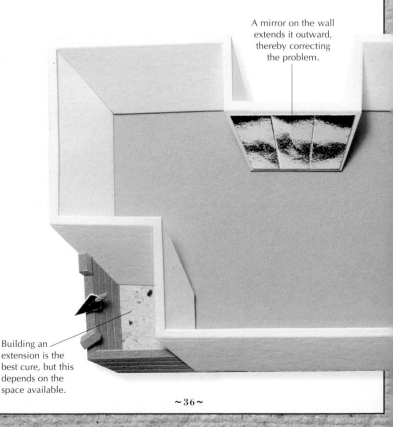

A mirror on the wall extends it outward, thereby correcting the problem.

Building an extension is the best cure, but this depends on the space available.

Missing corners mean the home will be lacking in certain luck aspects. What type of luck is missing depends on the compass directions of missing sectors. If one missing sector represents your nien yen direction, you can correct the situation in the following ways.

▨ Install a light.
▨ Hang a wall mirror.
▨ Build an extension.

What you do depends on your personal circumstances and whether you have the available space.

Having irregular-shaped layouts sometimes makes it difficult to arrange for the bedroom to be located in your best corner. If you cannot get the right location, tapping the nien yen direction is often good enough. This means you sleep with your head pointed to your nien yen direction. If you cannot tap either the location or direction, do try sleeping with the head pointed to at least one of your three other auspicious directions.

THE SLEEPING DIRECTION

This is one of the most vital determinants of good family luck. Try always to sleep with your head pointed to your nien yen direction. This not only ensures a harmonious and happy family life, but it also enhances your children's luck tremendously. The children do not just do well at school or at work, they are also obedient and dutiful, and bring honor to the family name. The direction your head points to when you sleep is vital!

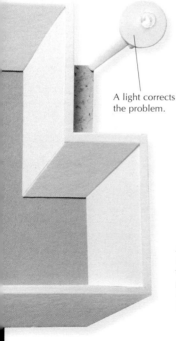

A light corrects the problem.

An irregularly shaped house may make it difficult to locate the main bedroom in the best place to ensure family luck. However, it is possible to improve the situation.

EAST AND WEST GROUP DIRECTIONS

Compass feng shui divides the human race into either east or west group people. Each person is said to have four favorable directions, each representing a different kind of auspicious luck. In addition to the family luck direction, therefore, you have three other auspicious directions. All these favorable directions belong to the same east or west group, so it is easy to surmise what your three good directions are.

What group you belong to depends on your personal Kua number. East group people have Kua numbers one, three, four, and nine.

West group people have the Kua numbers two, five, six, seven, and eight. Favorable east group directions are east, north, south, and southeast. Auspicious west group directions are west, southwest, northwest, and northeast.

NOTE

East group directions are bad for west group people and west group directions are harmful for east group people. This is also true of locations.

KUA NUMBER east/west group	Ho Hai direction	Wu Kwei direction
1 east group	West	Northeas
2 west group	East	Southeas
3 east group	Southwest	Northwes
4 east group	Northwest	Southwes
5 west group for males	East	Southeas
5 west group for females	South	North
6 west group	Southeast	East
7 west group	North	South
8 west group	South	North
9 east group	Northeast	West

SE	S	SW
E		W
NE	N	NW

If your Kua number is eight, your Kua chart will look like this, with the inauspicious directions marked in blue and the auspicious directions marked in red.

Lui Shar direction	Chueh Ming direction
Northwest	Southwest
South	North
Northeast	West
West	Northeast
South	North
East	Southeast
North	South
Southeast	East
East	Southeast
Southwest	Northwest

YOUR UNLUCKY DIRECTIONS

The compass formula also tells you the directions that can hurt you and your family. These four bad directions are different for each of the Kua numbers and they vary in the intensity of bad luck they bring to you and your family.

▨ The Ho Hai direction brings misfortune to the family in the form of illness and grievances.

▨ The Wu Kwei direction brings five ghosts to your doorstep. Harm could befall your family.

▨ The Lui Shar direction attacks you with six killings. Your family is plagued with bad luck.

▨ The Chueh Mung direction is the most severe of all. It means total loss of descendants.

The table on the left shows you the four harmful directions according to your own personal Kua number.

NOTE

It is important to remember your unlucky directions especially when orienting the main front door into your home, as well as your sleeping and sitting directions. Try drawing out your personalized Kua chart as shown above.

SAFEGUARDING YOUR CHILDREN'S HEALTH

保護 Feng shui offers useful guidelines on the placement of bedrooms and arrangement of furniture. This will ensure that your children are not being inadvertently hit by shar chi, which causes constant sickness. If your child frequently succumbs to viruses and infection, take a good look at the bedroom and check that the placement of the bed follows the simple principles outlined on this page.

PLACEMENT OF THE BED

In addition to the features shown, the bed should never be placed directly beneath an overhead beam. This is severely harmful. It should not be placed directly in front of the door in either direction. Always keep the bed clear of the door, especially if the door itself faces another door, a staircase, a mirror, or a toilet.

When there are several children in a household, try to avoid having bedrooms along a long corridor. Too many doors opening off a corridor can cause quarrels between siblings. Doors facing each other also cause arguments.

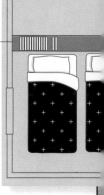

Sleeping with the headboard against a wall with a toilet on the other side is especially harmful to health. Do try to avoid having this kind of placement for the bed. According to feng shui, even if the head is pointing to the sleeper's best direction, harmful shar chi created in the toilet will cause ill health. Sleeping directly underneath a toilet on the upper floor is equally harmful.

Open bookshelves above a headboard cause the sleeper to have headaches and insomnia.

A dressing table with a mirror facing the bed is not advisable. Remove the mirror. The rule is never to sleep with a mirror facing the bed. In children's bedrooms, this can cause sickness.

The bed, placed diagonally to the door, is excellent. The position is also good in relation to the windows.

The regular shape of the bedroom is good. Try to avoid putting your children in triangular, odd, or L-shaped bedrooms.

Harmful shar chi emanating from the corner pillar is not hurting the bed. Never place the bed directly in the path of the sharp edge of this kind of pillar.

A desk next to the headboard is not advisable, and the door behind is not considered healthy.

The bed should be placed directly against a wall, not floating in the middle of the room.

A bed placed directly in line with the door is harmful, and it is worse if there is a window directly facing the door.

IMPROVING SCHOOL GRADES

Perhaps the most exciting promise of feng shui is its potential to create living spaces that encourage and motivate children to perform to the best of their ability. Study skills and attitudes improve substantially when children work in a harmoniously balanced environment.

THE SITTING DIRECTION

The first thing to do is to position the work desk in a way that makes your child face his or her best study direction. Grades are almost certain to improve, and he or she will become far more motivated and focused in his or her studies. This method uses the Kua compass formula. Use your child's year of birth (adjusted to the Chinese calendar), and work out his or her Kua number according to the formula given on page 29, then check the best study direction from the table here. Whenever the child is working, he or she should sit facing the best study direction. It will enhance learning ability and memory because the surrounding energies will be harmonious and auspicious.

Your Kua number is:	Your Study orientation is:
1	**NORTH** for both males and females
2	**SOUTHWEST** for both males and females
3	**EAST** for both males and females
4	**SOUTHEAST** for both males and females
5	**SOUTHWEST** for males and **NORTHEAST** for females
6	**NORTHWEST** for both males and females
7	**WEST** for both males and females
8	**NORTHEAST** for both males and females
9	**SOUTH** for both males and females

Never let your child sit below a toilet located on the upper floor. Make certain nothing sharp or pointed, such as the edge of a closet or a protruding corner, is hitting at the chair where your child is working. This creates shar chi, which harms the child. Also make sure that there are no beams or edges above.

He or she should sit with the head facing the best study direction and solid support behind. A painting of a mountain is excellent. Do not position the desk so that the window is directly behind it; this symbolizes a lack of support.

This auspicious direction method can be applied in other situations. Let your child face this direction when doing his or her homework, when sitting for an examination, in class, or when revising if at all possible. It is important to remember, however, that the luck of the good direction is no protection against shar chi caused by beams, pillars, and sharp edges, so you must make sure that you always avoid these structures.

Finally, this direction can also be activated during mealtimes. Allocate seats at the family table according to the different auspicious directions of each of the children in the family.

Staring at a dead tree trunk that is too near the window is extremely harmful. However, if there is a healthy-looking tree with foliage, and the direction outside is the east, it is most auspicious. Staring at a lamppost is almost as bad as looking out at a dead tree. Block it off with drapes.

PROTECTING CHILDREN AGAINST SHAR CHI

The defensive dimension of feng shui should never be ignored. Even if you get everything else correct, the killing breath of symbolic poison arrows, or shar chi, is extremely harmful and, in certain circumstances, it can even be lethal. Sleeping and sitting arrangements have already been covered, but, in addition, you should look out for features within the home and in the surrounding environment, which could be causing severe problems.

Symbolic poison arrows are always created when anything sharp or pointed is directly facing you. Thus, if your child, sitting at his or her desk, looks out of the window and is directly facing an oncoming road, a dead tree, or the edge of a large building, these structures can be the source of severe shar chi. Heavy drapes will help to block out the view, if there is no other alternative.

If your child's window directly faces a
road, as if the road were coming at the
room, the lights of cars at night would be
like tigers attacking in the dark. Tall
buildings are also hostile. This sort of view
could be harmful if the buildings are too
near. If they are far away, however, the
bad chi will have dissolved by the time
it reaches the window.

MAINTAINING YIN AND YANG BALANCE IN ROOMS

Another dimension of feng shui is the need to maintain yin and yang balance. These are the two primordial forces that are opposite and yet complementary. Good feng shui can only exist when the two forces are correctly in balance.

To understand about yin and yang balance, it is important to realize that one gives existence to the other. Thus yin is darkness, night, cold, quiet, and stillness. Yang, on the other hand, is daylight, brightness, warmth, sounds, and activity. Thus, without cold, there is no warmth, and without sunshine, there can be no night time. Another attribute of the yin and yang cosmology is that one contains the seed of the other. Thus, in yang there must always be some yin and vice versa.

In feng shui, yin and yang balance requires the presence of both forces, but because we are dealing with life and energy when we speak of good feng shui, the environment should never be too yin. This creates lethargy and even death, yet it is necessary not to do away with yin altogether. Maintaining good balance between the two forces in feng shui requires great care and forethought.

The major directions of the home that affect children's luck are the east and the west. Make certain that the space that represents these two directions never gets too yin, for children's luck needs the energy, light, and life of yang.

This side of the home is completely overwhelmed. There is a high fence encroaching on the house, an overhanging roof which casts a shadow, and trees that have grown thick with foliage. Remove or lower the fence and thin out the trees to let in the sunlight!

A bright, cheerful room will attract positive energies and help your child to grow and develop.

Outside the home this happens when trees are allowed to grow out of hand, thereby completely blocking out the sunlight. When there is no sunshine, the environment becomes unhealthy. If the foliage of the trees creates excessive shade and darkness, the situation has definitely become too yin, to an extent that it may become harmful. Trim the trees and, if there are too many, thin them by cutting some down. This lets in the sunlight. Never allow trees outside the window of your children's rooms to block out the sun entirely. This causes sickness and, worse, lethargy, and depression.

Inside the home, space becomes too yin when rooms are damp and cold. This usually happens when store rooms or unoccupied rooms are not properly maintained. Never allow rooms to stay dark, cold, and damp for long periods. It is never good feng shui for the home and the first to be affected are usually the children of the household.

Children's rooms should have a good amount of yang energy. This is conducive to healthy growth and development. Paint the room in happy, bright colors. Install a music system or hang little chimes that make tinkling sounds.

Do not hang pictures or paintings of hostile faces or wild animals. The spirit of the predator is considered to be very real when symbols that depict it are present, so avoid such animals as tigers, leopards, and lions. The tiger is especially to be feared. Feng shui always warns against hanging pictures of them inside the home. They are excellent when hung outside the home, but there are very few people who can take the tiger into the house.

Keep pictures of tigers and other wild animals outside the home.

~ 47 ~

HARMONY
AMONG SIBLINGS

ARRANGEMENT OF ROOMS

妙
妹

How rooms are placed in relation to each other and how
doors face each other has feng
shui consequences. If they are
placed correctly, siblings get
along and there is goodwill
between them. Where
these have feng shui faults, it is
much more likely that
quarrels and misunder-
standings will prevail.

A bedroom placed
next to a toilet is
seldom auspicious.

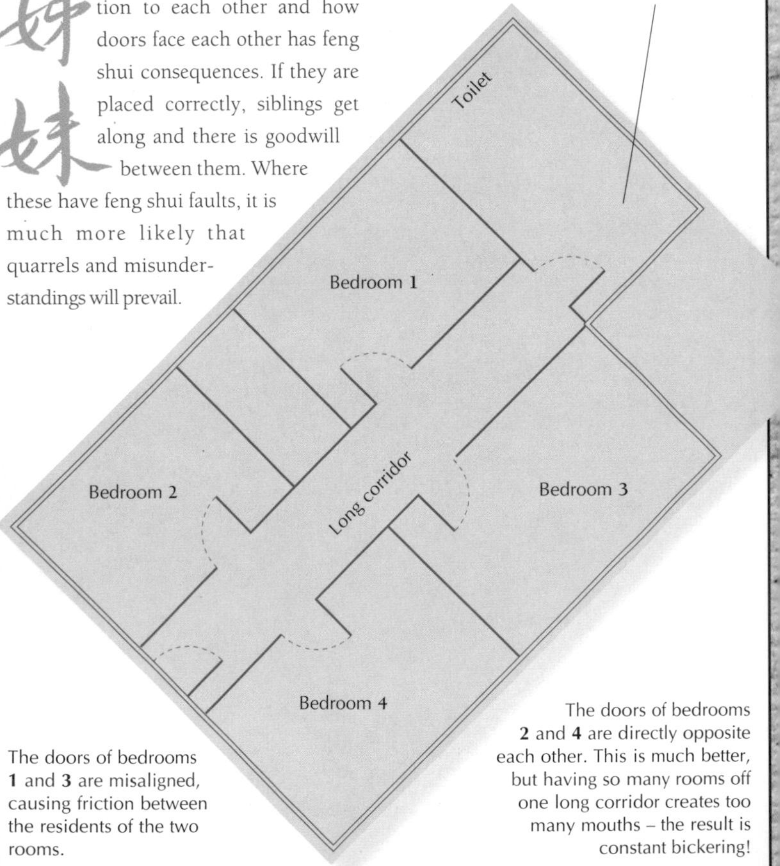

Toilet

Bedroom 1

Bedroom 2

Long corridor

Bedroom 3

Bedroom 4

The doors of bedrooms
1 and **3** are misaligned,
causing friction between
the residents of the two
rooms.

The doors of bedrooms
2 and **4** are directly opposite
each other. This is much better,
but having so many rooms off
one long corridor creates too
many mouths – the result is
constant bickering!

OTHER UNFORTUNATE ARRANGEMENTS

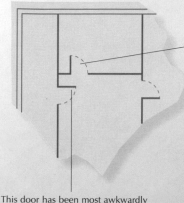

The hinges of this door have been fixed in a way that causes feng shui problems. Change the hinges, otherwise anyone occupying this room will be unable to get along with the rest of the household.

Doors should be the same size.

This door has been most awkwardly placed. It opens outward instead of inward. This indicates the occupant of this room cannot stay at home and cannot get along with his or her siblings. It is also blocking the other door, thereby affecting the feng shui of the occupant of the other room.

SIZE OF BEDS

Unlikely as this may seem, many parents allow their children to sleep on beds that are either far too large or small for their children. Tall children sleeping on beds that are too short will suffer from constant illness. Different size beds for different children causes hidden resentments and jealousies among siblings. Get beds that are in proportion to your children's physique and allow them room to grow.

SIZE OF DOORS

Doors that are next to, or near, each other should be of the same dimensions. If one is larger or taller, the occupant of the room with the bigger door will have a tendency to bully or dominate the resident of the other room.

FEATURES THAT HURT CHILDREN

In their eagerness to practice feng shui, many people simply do not understand that they could well make tiny mistakes that have major consequences and these consequences often do not become immediately apparent. While it is generally known that water is good wealth feng shui, one great danger of activating it in the house, for example, is when it is placed under the staircase. This is a major taboo in feng shui. Never place any kind of water feature – a waterfall, fountain, or fish pond – under the staircase of the home. This destroys the luck of the second generation. Water under the staircase brings tragic consequences to the children of the household.

A water feature underneath the staircase hurts the children
of the family. If you wish to decorate this area, place
something solid here. This gives foundation to the home.

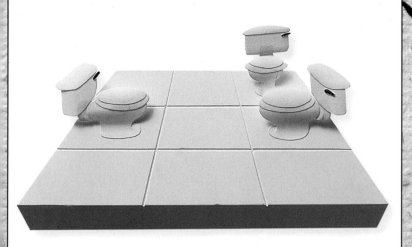

The position of toilets could affect the
future prospects of the children of the house.

TOILETS IN THE WRONG PLACES

If the toilet is in the southwest, it seriously blocks the marriage opportunities for the next generation. It will be difficult for the younger generation to find life partners. If the toilet is used by visitors, the effect is even more severe and girls in the family could well end up remaining spinsters. This feature also has very damaging effects on the marriage of the older generation.

A toilet in the west, which is of the metal element, causes general bad luck for your children. This is the corner that represents children's luck. Flushing the water away is especially harmful here because metal produces water – the metal element will become seriously exhausted.

The presence of a toilet in the east spoils the luck of the sons of the family, especially the eldest. In this corner, which is of the wood element, the effect of flushing away the water is even worse than in the west because water actually produces wood. It is like depriving the wood element of sustenance. The boys of the family get hurt and the health of the family will also suffer.

The best way of dealing with a toilet in the wrong place is to keep it closed. Better still, create some kind of divider that blocks off a view of the toilet. Small toilets are strongly recommended. In the old days, Chinese homes did not have toilets. This is because wherever they are located, they affect some kind of luck.

THE TIME DIMENSION

USING FLYING STAR FENG SHUI

時
間

This formula addresses the changes in feng shui over a period of time. This popular method is widely used in Hong Kong, Malaysia, and Singapore. The time aspects of feng shui complement the space dimension of other feng shui methods. Flying star thus adds the vital dynamics of the time factor. This is a very advanced method and it is not really necessary for amateur practitioners to get too involved in the technical details of its computations. However, it is useful to have a reference table to enable you to investigate the impact of flying star on your own feng shui, particularly since this method is excellent for warning against the flying stars that bring serious bad luck. Being forewarned is often a great way of avoiding bad luck.

WHAT ARE THE FLYING STARS?

The stars refer to the numbers one to nine placed around a nine-sector grid, known as the Lo Shu magic square. The numbers around the grid fly – they change over time. The way they do this forms the crux of this method of feng shui.

Every day, month, and year, and every 20-year period has its own arrangement of numbers around the square. Every number has its own meanings and tells the feng shui expert, who knows how to interpret the numbers, a great many things. For the purpose of getting warnings, it is sufficient to monitor the period and year stars.

SOUTH

4	9	2
3	5	7
8	1	6

THE PERIOD OF SEVEN

We are currently living through the period of seven, which started in 1984 and does not end until the year 2003. This means that during this period, the number seven is deemed to be very lucky. The Lo Shu square for this period is shown here. Through an interpretation of the numbers, it describes the fortunate and less fortunate sectors up to the year 2003.

SOUTH

6	2	4
5	7	9
1	3	8

The original nine-sector Lo Shu square has the number five in the center. The numbers have been arranged so that the sum of any three numbers, taken vertically, horizontally, or diagonally, is 15. In flying star feng shui, the numbers move from grid to grid and they are then interpreted according to which of them is in which square. Each of the eight sectors on the outside of the square represents a corner of the home. For analysis, the center is the ninth sector. South is placed at the top according to tradition, for presentation purposes only. Use a compass to identify the actual corners of your home.

During the period of seven, the bad-luck star number five is located in the east. This is interpreted to mean that if the main door of your home is located in the east, you should be very careful during this 20-year period. It also means that those sleeping in bedrooms located in the east should also be extra careful against being stabbed in the back.

The analysis will be more accurate when investigation is also conducted on the star numerals during the month and the year in question. When two or all three star numerals are fives in the same sector, loss due to extreme bad luck is certain during that month and year for anyone whose bedroom is in the sector where the fives occur together! When you become aware of the time when you need to be extra careful, one way of countering the bad luck is to travel away from home. Go for a vacation during that period, thereby avoiding the bad luck.

Year	Star numeral 2 is in the	Star numeral 5 is in the
1997	Southeast	West
1998	Center	Northeast
1999	Northwest	South
2000	West	North
2001	Northeast	Southwest
2002	South	East
2003	North	Southeast
2004	Southwest	Center
2005	East	Northwest
2006	Southeast	West

Year	Month 1	Month 2	Month 3	Month 4	Month 5
1997	Southwest	East Northwest	Southeast West	Northeast	South Northwes
1998	Northeast	Northwest South	West North	Northeast Southwest	South East
1999	Northeast Southwest	South East	North Southeast	Southwest	East Northwes
2000	Southwest	East Northwest	Southeast West	Northeast	Northwe South
2001	Northeast	Northwest South	West North	Northeast Southwest	South East

ROOMS TO AVOID DURING SPECIFIC PERIODS

The yearly reference table
(*based on the lunar year)

The table opposite shows where the star five and star two occur together. The star two combined with five makes it extra dangerous. The two stars will also bring sickness.

THE MONTHLY REFERENCE TABLES.
(*based on the lunar months)

The table below indicates the dangerous sectors during each of the 12 lunar months over the next five years. These are the sectors where the star

Based on this reference table, rooms in the south are prone to sickness in 1999. In 2002 rooms in the south and east should be avoided, and in 2005 rooms in the east.

numerals two and five are located during that month. In the years 1998 and 2001 there are 13 lunar months, so one of the months has been doubled.

Match where the star numerals two and five fall during the months indicated with those of the annual star numerals and the 20-year period star numerals.

Where twos and fives occur together is when that sector becomes dangerous and anyone occupying a room in an afflicted sector would do well to leave it for that time. Be particularly careful when the star numerals two and five fall into the east sector. This is because this is the sector afflicted with the five in the 20-year period flying star. The danger months and the directions are marked. When there are two dots, it means that both the sectors indicated are dangerous.

Month 6	Month 7	Month 8	Month 9	Month 10	Month 11	Month 12
West North	Northeast Southwest	South East	North Southeast	Southwest	East Northwest	Southeast West
South East	North Southeast	Southwest	East Northwest	Southeast West	Northeast	Northwest South
Southeast West	Northeast	Northwest South	West North	Northeast Southwest	South East	North Southeast
West North	Northeast Southwest	South East	North Southeast	Southwest	East Northwest	Southeast West
North Southeast	Southwest	East Northwest	Southeast West	Northeast	Northwest South	West North

INDEX

FURTHER READING

Kwok, Man-Ho and O'Brien, Joanne,
The Elements of Feng Shui,
ELEMENT BOOKS, SHAFTESBURY, 1991

Lo, Raymond *Feng Shui: The Pillars of
Destiny (Understanding Your Fate and
Fortune),* TIMES EDITIONS, SINGAPORE, 1995

Skinner, Stephen, *Living Earth Manual
of Feng Shui: Chinese Geomancy,*
PENGUIN, 1989

Too, Lillian, *Basic Feng Shui,*
KONSEP BOOKS, KUALA LUMPUR, 1997

Too, Lillian, *The Complete Illustrated
Guide to Feng Shui,* ELEMENT BOOKS,
SHAFTESBURY, 1996

Too, Lillian, *Chinese Astrology for
Romance and Relationships,*
KONSEP BOOKS, KUALA LUMPUR, 1996

Too, Lillian *Chinese Numerology
in Feng Shui,* KONSEP BOOKS,
KUALA LUMPUR, 1994

Too, Lillian, *Dragon Magic,*
KONSEP BOOKS, KUALA LUMPUR, 1996

Too, Lillian *Feng Shui,* KONSEP BOOKS,
KUALA LUMPUR, 1993

Too, Lillian *Practical Applications for
Feng Shui,* KONSEP BOOKS,
KUALA LUMPUR, 1994

Too, Lillian *Water Feng Shui for Wealth,*
KONSEP BOOKS, KUALA LUMPUR, 1995

Walters, Derek *Feng Shui Handbook:
A Practical Guide to Chinese Geomancy
and Environmental Harmony,*
AQUARIAN PRESS, 1991

USEFUL ADDRESSES

Feng Shui Design Studio
PO Box 705, Glebe, Sydney, NSW 2037,
Australia, Tel: 61 2 315 8258

Feng Shui Society of Australia
PO Box 1565, Rozelle, Sydney
NSW 2039, Australia

The Geomancer
The Feng Shui Store
PO Box 250, Woking, Surrey GU21 1YJ
Tel: 44 1483 839898
Fax: 44 1483 488998

Feng Shui Association
31 Woburn Place, Brighton BN1 9GA,
Tel/Fax: 44 1273 693844

Feng Shui Network International
PO Box 2133, London W1A 1RL,
Tel: 44 171 935 8935,
Fax: 44 171 935 9295

The School of Feng Shui
34 Banbury Road, Ettington,
Stratford-upon-Avon, Warwickshire
CV37 7SU. Tel/Fax: 44 1789 740116

The Feng Shui Institute of America
PO Box 488, Wabasso, FL 32970,
Tel: 1 407 589 9900 Fax: 1 407 589 1611

Feng Shui Warehouse
PO Box 3005, San Diego, CA 92163,
Tel: 1 800 399 1599 Fax: 1 800 997 9831

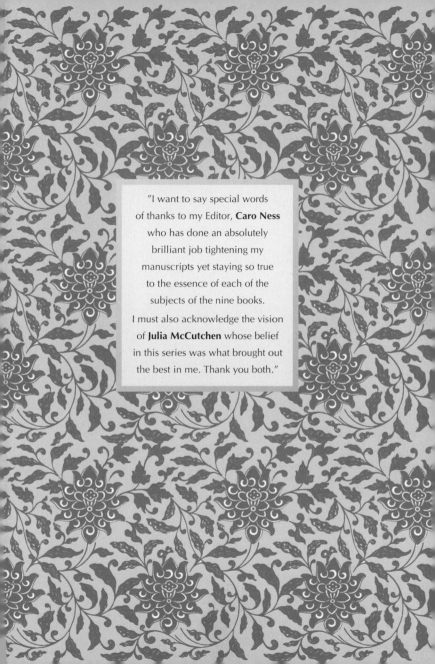

"I want to say special words of thanks to my Editor, **Caro Ness** who has done an absolutely brilliant job tightening my manuscripts yet staying so true to the essence of each of the subjects of the nine books.
I must also acknowledge the vision of **Julia McCutchen** whose belief in this series was what brought out the best in me. Thank you both."

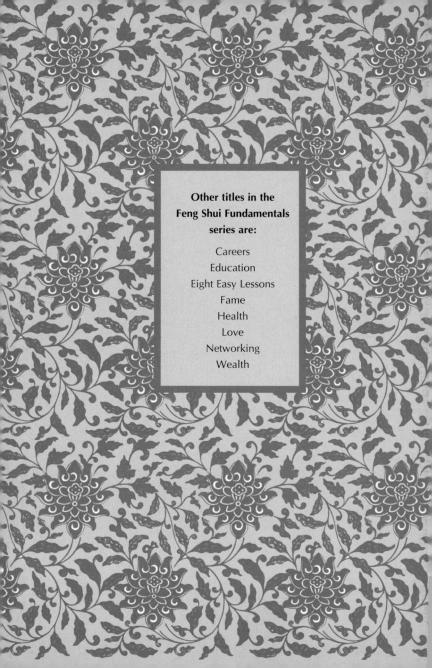